BOOK ANALYSIS

By Jule Lenzen

The Other Boleyn Girl

by Philippa Gregory

PHILIPPA GREGORY

ENGLISH NOVELIST

- **Born in Nairobi, Kenya in 1954.**
- **Notable works:**
  - *A Respectable Trade* (1995), novel
  - *The Boleyn Inheritance* (2006), novel
  - *The White Queen* (2009), novel

Philippa Gregory is a historian, writer and broadcaster. She holds a PhD in 18th-century literature from the University of Edinburgh. Previously, she graduated in History from the University of Sussex. She is a Regent for the University of Edinburgh, an honorary fellow of the Universities of Sussex and Cardiff and holds an honorary degree from Teesside University. In 1993 she founded the charity Gardens for The Gambia.

Her novels are set in historical contexts, often revolving around British royal history. She has also written fictional stories within a historical setting, such as *A Respectable Trade*, which tells of the love story between an English girl and her black servant in 18th-century Bristol. Her most recent publication is *Dark Tracks*, the fourth volume in a historical series set in the 1500s, revolving around the expansion of the Ottoman Empire into Europe.

THE OTHER BOLEYN GIRL

WOMEN'S DANGEROUS LIVES AT THE ENGLISH TUDOR COURT

- **Genre:** historical novel
- **Reference edition:** Gregory, P. (2017) *The Other Boleyn Girl*. London: Harper.
- **1st edition:** 2001
- **Themes:** British royal history, Tudors, intrigue, power, betrayal, sisterly rivalry, female development, love

Anne Boleyn is a well-known name in British history, as the second wife of Henry VIII. Less well known is the name of her sister Mary: she was the king's mistress before Anne, and, according to Gregory, even bore him two children. Gregory explores this part of history from the perspective of Mary Carey (née Boleyn) in her novel *The Other Boleyn Girl*. Gregory spent three years researching before writing the story (Chrisafis, 2002: n.p.). The novel was immensely popular and won the Romantic Novel of the Year Award in 2002. Its historical accuracy is disputed, however.

SUMMARY

The book starts out as it ends: with a beheading. Mary is 13, already married and is present at the beheading of her uncle, the Duke of Buckinghamshire. She believes that the king will pardon his prisoner at the last moment, but he does not. One year later, in 1522, Mary is a lady in waiting at the court of Queen Katherine, Princess of Spain and Queen of England. Her father brings her sister Anne, who was educated abroad, at the French Court, back to court.

MARY'S AFFAIR WITH THE KING

The king takes a shine to Mary, and she is pushed by her family to start an affair with him. This lasts from 1522 to 1527. Mary is at first reluctant, being married already, but eventually gives in under the pressure of her family. Henry showers her with gifts: a new horse, new gowns, and titles and wealth for the members of her family. George, her brother and advisor to the king, is the one who always escorts her to and from the king's rooms. The king is increasingly worried that his queen might not give him a son and heir. This is why the family encourages the affair between Mary and Henry – if she bears him a son, the family will rise in his favour and the boy might eventually be the king of England. Mary falls pregnant, and gives birth to a daughter who she names Catherine in honour of the queen. The baby is taken away from her soon after, and she longs to be with her. At the same time, Anne has fallen in love with a nobleman at court, Henry Percy. He is the heir of the Duke of Northumberland and therefore higher in status than Anne. They marry in secret and consummate the marriage. Henry Percy's father is against the marriage, as is the Boleyn/Howard family, and it is annulled against Anne and Henry's wishes. Mary starts spending her summers at the family seat in Kent, Hever. She again falls pregnant, and this time she gives birth to a boy, Henry. During her pregnancy and lying-in (during the last month of the pregnancy, women were required to lie in a darkened room), the Boleyn/Howard family do not want the king's attention to stray from their family, and therefore command Anne to keep the king entertained.

ANNE'S AFFAIR WITH THE KING

Anne has always been ambitious, and she made it clear from the beginning of the novel that she would never settle for being the king's mistress. While he falls deeper and deeper in love with her, she keeps him at arm's length. They plot together to set the old queen aside, as she is now barren and cannot bear Henry a male heir. They plan to have the marriage annulled on the grounds that she was Henry's brother's wife before, and it was against God's will that he should have married her at all. While Anne is the king's constant companion during the day, Mary is sent for during the night to satisfy the king's sexual desires, and to prevent him from straying to other families. In the summer months, Mary always visits Hever, where she spends time with her children. After the king sets her aside, she and her husband, William Carey, slowly get to know each other again and become lovers. In 1528 there is an outbreak of an illness, the sweat, and Anne fights for her life but survives. Mary's husband dies. Anne plots to adopt Mary's son, Henry, so that the king will get a new wife and an heir in one, in marrying her.

ANNE AS QUEEN OF ENGLAND

After six years of conducting an affair, Henry finally overrules the Catholic Church, declares himself head of the new Church of England and marries Anne. She is disliked by the people for having overruled Queen Katherine, who by this time lives in exile on an estate, and Anne's coronation is conducted without any cheers from the public. To begin with, the marriage between Henry and Anne seems to be a good match. Anne falls pregnant, but instead of the hoped-for boy, she gives birth to a girl, the Princess Elizabeth. During her pregnancy, Henry's attention wavers from her and he takes a new mistress, another Howard girl. Anne is displeased by this and her life is more and more characterised by the constant fear of being supplanted, and the desperate desire to give birth to a boy.

Meanwhile, Mary still spends her summers in Hever and is often accompanied by William Stafford, one of the men who works for her uncle. In name and rank he is far below her, but he nevertheless woos her. He promises her a simple life, as a farmer's wife, far away from court. On a court trip to Calais, they become lovers (although they do not sleep with one another), but William wants to marry and Mary feels too bound to the wishes of her family to accept. William leaves the court. Mary realises that she wants to spend her life with him and follows him to his farm, where they get married. They return to court, but do not tell anyone about their marriage.

Anne gives birth to several dead babies, and George and Mary help to cover up her miscarriages in order to avoid the gossip of the court. Henry drifts further and further away from Anne, who, in her desperation, sleeps with her brother George to finally give birth to a boy. When Mary falls pregnant by her husband William, Anne bans her from court for disobeying her wishes. Mary gives birth to a girl, and when Anne is pregnant, she is welcomed back to court. It becomes apparent that Henry detests his wife, and he finally devises a plan to get rid of her. He courts Jane Seymour, and Anne is sent to the Tower. Mary's daughter Catherine accompanies Anne. Until the last moment, Mary does not want to believe that Henry will behead Anne; however, Anne is executed in 1536.

CHARACTER STUDY

MARY CAREY (NÉE BOLEYN)

At the beginning of the novel, Mary is but a young girl, however, she is already married. Throughout the novel, she blooms into a woman and mother. Mary is the youngest of the three Boleyn siblings: she has an older sister, Anne, and an older brother, George. She is married to William Carey at the age of 12. He dies in 1528, when Mary is 20. She is fair-haired, the complete opposite to her sister Anne. During her marriage to Carey, Mary is ordered by her family to become the king's mistress, and she obeys. She bears him a daughter, Catherine, in 1524 and a son, Henry, in 1526. Mary is devoted to Queen Katherine and hates the part she has to play in her betrayal (p. 250).

She enjoys spending her summer at the family seat in Kent, Hever, and dreams of a simple life. She knows her place and is submissive to the wishes of her family – she tries to speak up for herself a few times but is too afraid of the power her family has over her. Her true act of defiance is her marrying William Stafford for love, rather than status.

Mary is very naïve and sometimes a bit slow in catching up with current politics (p. 328), but she has a good heart. She is characterised as pretty, sweet and innocent in the beginning (p. 7), and she is exceedingly honest: "I would have confessed to the family's plot to ensnare him but for Anne, waiting in the shadows of the jousting tent." (p. 30). This honesty is partly grounded in her innocence. In time, though, she grows accustomed to the falsity of the court and puts on a show while she is there (p. 160).

There is an extensive rivalry between the sisters, sometimes bordering on hatred (p. 180). Although the narrative is told mostly from Mary's perspective, the reader gets the impression that Anne Boleyn is the main character, as she is by far the more dominant of the two.

ANNE BOLEYN

Anne, from the beginning of the novel, is a grown woman. She returns to the English court after having been educated at the French court, and she has adopted French manners and style. (p. 6) She is the complete opposite of Mary, in character as well as in looks: dark-haired, she is defiant, seductive, witty and self-confident.

She is also prone to temperamental and violent outbursts (p. 180), mean-spirited and jealous (p. 162). She is extremely bossy and selfish, and only works for her own benefit. These negative character traits are only enhanced once she is queen: she treats her family members with disdain even though they have helped her to this place of power and she sees herself as invincible. Anne seems heartless and cold in this regard: she adopts Mary's beloved son (p. 243) and poisons everyone who stands in her way. She also treats the 'old' queen in a disdainful way.

As she is very calculating, she knows exactly how to get what she wants, which is to be Queen of England. She would do anything to achieve this aim, and so even sleeps with her brother George in order to finally conceive a male heir for the country. However, her cunning and selfishness are eventually her downfall: Henry tires of her games and seeks to replace her. In 1536, she is be-headed on the Tower Green. Until the very end, she keeps a hold over Mary – as her accompaniment to the Tower, she chooses Mary's daughter Catherine. She also never tires of reminding Mary that her son is Anne's ward (p. 249).

Before setting her sights on Henry and the Crown of England, Anne conducts a brief love affair with Henry Percy, the heir of the Duke of Northumberland. She seems to love him and losing him breaks her heart. She says herself that after this point, she is only driven by ambition, not love (p. 129).

HENRY VIII

Henry is portrayed as a selfish, childish man, with an easily wavering attention. It seems like the entire court and particularly the women can guide him whichever way they want him to go: even though he is the official head of the country, he does not seem to notice how the powerful families around him, such as the Boleyns or the Seymours, guide his actions.

He is extremely influenced by Anne, who convinces him to found the Church of England. In the end, he becomes a tyrant: he is not only head of the country, but head of the Church, and believes his whims and thoughts to be God-given.

King Henry is desperate for a son, a male heir, a wish that guides all of his actions. He is also prone to temperamental outbursts, and anyone who angers or disobeys him loses his favour, be it his lover Mary, his wife Queen Katherine or one of his advisors.

At the beginning of the novel, Henry is still married to the much older Spanish Princess, Queen Katherine. They have a daughter, Princess Mary, together. In 1533, after many years of trying to annul his marriage with the now barren Queen Katherine, Henry marries Anne Boleyn. They have another daughter, Princess Elizabeth. As Anne does not bear him any more children, he eventually turns to Jane Seymour, who will become his third wife once Anne is beheaded.

Henry is young and handsome at the beginning of the novel. In 1536, however, he incurs a wound on his leg during a jousting tournament, which cripples him and makes him even more foul-tempered. He grows fat and ugly, and, being exceedingly vain, this does nothing to add to his goodwill.

ANALYSIS

GENRE: HISTORICAL NOVEL

- The first historical novel was *Waverley* (1814) by Sir Walter Scott.
- The historical novel "attempts to convey the spirit, manners, and social conditions of a past age with realistic detail and fidelity (which is in some cases only apparent fidelity) to historical fact" (*Encyclopaedia Britannica*, 2013)
- The novel either deals with actual historical personages or a mixture of historical and fictional characters.
- It may be written to high literary standard or be a costume romance that merely uses a past setting for adventurous purposes.

The Other Boleyn Girl contains several passages that underline its historical setting and serve to demonstrate in-depth historical knowledge of the period:

> "The huntsman blew his horn and every horse in the courtyard stiffened with excitement. [...]

My mare, Jesmond, was like a coiled spring, and when the master of the hunt led the way over the drawbridge we trotted quickly after him, the hounds like a sea of brindle and white around the horses' hooves. [...] the haymakers leant on their scythes and watched us pass, doffing their caps as they saw the bright colours of the aristocratic riders, and then dropping to their knees as they saw the king's standard." (p. 64)

It deals with actual historical personages rather than with a mixture of historical and fictional characters. The main characters are all members of the royal Tudor court and historically attested. There is even historical evidence for the minor characters, such as Mark Smeaton, who eventually betrays Anne to Secretary Cromwell.

HISTORICAL CONTEXT AND ACCURACY

Henry VIII was probably the most famous king in England's history. He reigned from 1509 to 1547 and was married six times: first to Katherine of Aragon, whom he divorced, second to Anne Boleyn, whom he had beheaded, and third to Jane Seymour, who gave him his first and only male heir and who died in childbed. He was then briefly betrothed to Anne of Cleves, whom he divorced, then to Catherine Howard, a relative of the Boleyn sisters who was also beheaded for adultery, and, finally, to Catherine Parr, who survived him.

Apart from his six marriages, he is famous for breaking away from the Roman Catholic Church and founding the Church of England. Ironically, the child who ruled England most successfully and who a whole period is named after is his and Anne's daughter Elizabeth, who became Elizabeth I.

Of Mary Boleyn, the sister of Anne Boleyn, little is known, and Gregory's novel is an attempt to change this. However, the historical accuracy of Gregory's novel is debated. According to her own website, "Her love for history and commitment to historical accuracy are the hallmarks of her writing." (Gregory: n.p.). However, not all elements of her novel are founded on truth. Obviously, a historical novel to an extent presents an interpretation of characters, as historical sources usually only hint at their personalities. Female characters in particular are neglected in historical documents, and so the author has the freedom to invent the character for themselves.

However, Gregory's portrayal of Anne Boleyn in particular is cause for controversy: Gregory paints her as a very negative character, cunning, violent and seductive. Hilary Mantel, another historical author, points out that there is no evidence for Anne's having been a seductress (Mantel, 2012: n.p.). She goes on to state that Anne "[...] takes on the colour of our fantasies and is shaped by our preoccupations: witch, bitch, feminist, sexual temptress, cold opportunist." (*ibid*.).

Moreover, several incidents that Gregory presents as facts are not historically proven: it is unclear whether, for example, Anne Boleyn ever gave birth to a deformed foetus – this story might have sprung from propaganda against her daughter Elizabeth I (*ibid*.). Other details of the novel are historically attested, however, such as Anne's dancing in yellow upon Queen Katherine's death. (*ibid*.).

When David Starkey, a historian, appeared alongside Gregory in a BBC documentary on

Anne Boleyn, he warned: "We really should stop taking historical novelists seriously as historians [...] The idea that they have authority is ludicrous. They are very good at imagining character: that's why the novels sell. They have no authority when it comes to the handling of historical sources. Full stop." (Davies, 2013: n.p.).

Finally, the Tudor court Gregory creates in her novel seems to one-dimensionally revolve around sex: this evokes the feeling that a sensationalised portrayal is attempted, tailored to contemporary audiences rather than historical facts.

NARRATIVE DEVICES

In terms of narrative voice, the novel is mostly told from Mary's point of view in a first person narrative voice. However, at some points an omniscient narrator takes over, such as in the following passage: "Almost as soon as the French envoys were gone, as if he had been waiting for quietness and secrecy, Cardinal Wolsey created a hidden court of law and summoned witnesses, prosecutors, and defendants." (p. 199). The same passage later states that Mary is unaware of these proceedings.

From the beginning, certain overarching themes are played out, foreshadowing events that take place later in the book. One of these themes is Queen Katherine's age – she is so much older than Henry that she grows barren and cannot give him his male heir. When she first appears at court, Anne already highlights this fact, which is especially potent coming from her mouth as she will be the one to replace Queen Katherine eventually:

> "'Ssshhh,' I said reprovingly. 'She's a beautiful woman. The finest queen in Europe.' 'She's an old woman,' Anne said cruelly. 'Dressed like an old woman in the ugliest clothes of Europe, from the stupidest nation in Europe. We have no time for the Spanish.'" (p. 6)

Another overarching theme is the closeness between Anne and George. It is insinuated in various passages that the two of them share more than the common affection between siblings:

> "He leaned forward and kissed her again. Her eyes closed and her lips smiled and then parted. [...] I watched, quite fascinated and quite horrified, as his fingers went into her smooth dark hair and pulled her head back for his kiss. [...]

> George returned to his place at the fireside and we all pretended that it was nothing more than a brotherly kiss." (p. 309)

In another passage, George says: "[...] I'm her [Anne's] brother and I'd have her now. She could drive a man crazed" (p. 313). These passages foreshadow the incest between the two towards the end of the novel.

Foreshadowing also happens in the following scene, in which Anne, Mary and Henry Percy walk together:

> "'I think you would find that the Bible forbids it,' Anne said provocatively. 'The Bible orders a man to choose between sisters and to stay with his first choice. Anything else is cardinal sin.' Lord Henry Percy laughed. 'I'm sure I could get an indulgence,' he said. 'The Pope would surely grant me a dispensation. With two sisters like this, what man could be made to choose?'" (p. 88)

This is interesting in multiple ways: firstly, it foreshadows the king's interest in both Boleyn sisters. Secondly, Anne here argues that the Bible says a man should stay with his first choice. She will later argue for exactly the opposite in order to become queen. Should the king follow this logic, he would have had to stay with Mary as his first choice, rather than making Anne Queen of England. Finally, Henry Percy mentions the Pope in this context, which again foreshadows the dispensation King Henry later tries to get from the Pope, so as to be allowed to marry Anne.

Finally, George at one point says to Anne: "'Good God, Anne, if you ever leave court you could set up as a witch [...]. You have the gentleness already.'" (p. 161). This foreshadows the end of the novel, where repeated accusations of witchcraft lead to Henry's cooling towards Anne, and her eventual death.

FURTHER REFLECTION

SOME QUESTIONS TO THINK ABOUT...

- Who do you think is the true main character of the novel? The other Boleyn girl, Mary, as the title indicates? Or Anne? Explain your answer.
- Do you think the style of narration reflects the way the court revolves around the royal couple and the way in which, even though it is Mary's perspective, Anne's life still takes precedence?
- Leading on from the previous questions, what narrative and structural devices are employed to underline Mary's centrality to the plot?
- Many readers of Philippa Gregory prize her for her feminist endeavour in unearthing women whose stories have been disregarded in popular history. Would you say that the portrayal of Mary underlines a feminist intention? Consider the following exemplary quote in this context: "'She's a Boleyn and a Howard,' I said frankly. 'Underneath the great name, we're all bitches on heat.'" (p. 305).

- Do you think Anne always plotted to become Queen of England, even though she denies such an intention many times to her sister Mary? Consider their conversations on pp. 36-37 and p. 77 in this context.
- Gregory comments on the novel: "This is a story of a woman who overcame tyranny and patriarchy to dominate the royal court and eventually marry for love. My depiction of history is always very bleak and realistic." (Chrisafis, 2002: n.p.) Would you say that this is the most apparent message conveyed? And would you agree with her assertion of bleakness and realism?
- Compare the novel to the 2008 film adaption. The endings in particular differ – why do you think the changes were made, such as Anne and Mary seeing each other before Anne's death, and Mary begging for Anne's life?
- Given the controversy around Anne Boleyn, what could have prompted Gregory to portray her in such a negative light? Explain your answer.
- What do you think Gregory is trying to achieve with the constant foreshadowing of events in this novel?

We want to hear from you!
Leave a comment on your online library
and share your favourite books on social media!

FURTHER READING

REFERENCE EDITION

- Gregory, P. (2017) *The Other Boleyn Girl*. London: Harper.

REFERENCE STUDIES

- Chrisafis, A. (2002) Everyday story of courtly folk takes romantic fiction award. *The Guardian*. [Online]. [Accessed 22 January 2019]. Available from: <https://www.theguardian.com/uk/2002/apr/19/books.booksnews>

- Davies, S. (2013) David Starkey: it is 'ludicrous' to suggest that historical novelists have authority. *The Telegraph*. [Online]. [Accessed 22 January 2019]. Available from: <https://www.telegraph.co.uk/culture/tvandradio/10049866/David-Starkey-it-is-ludicrous-to-suggest-that-historical-novelists-have-authority.html>

- Gregory, P. (No date) *Biography*. [Online]. [Accessed 22 January 2019]. Available from: <https://www.philippagregory.com/biography>

- Gregory, P. (No date) *Behind Order of Darkness Volume IV – Dark Tracks*. [Online].

[Accessed 22 January 2019]. Available from: <https://www.philippagregory.com/books/order-of-darkness-volume-iv-dark-tracks/behind-the-book>

- (2013) Historical Novel. *Encyclopaedia Britannica*. [Online]. [Accessed 22 January 2019]. Available from: <https://www.britannica.com/art/historical-novel>

- Mantel, H. (2012) Anne Boleyn: witch, bitch, temptress, feminist. *The Guardian*. [Online]. [Accessed 23 January 2019]. Available from: <https://www.theguardian.com/books/2012/may/11/hilary-mantel-on-anne-boleyn>

- Morrill, J. S. and G. R. Elton. (2019) Henry VIII, King of England. *Encyclopaedia Britannica*. [Online]. [Accessed 24 January 2019]. Available from: <https://www.britannica.com/biography/Henry-VIII-king-of-England>

ADDITIONAL SOURCES

- Official website: www.philippagregory.com

- *The Last Days of Anne Boleyn*. (2013) [TV film]. Rob Coldstream. Dir. UK: BBC.

- Guy, J. (1988) *Tudor England*. Oxford: Oxford University Press.

- Lindsey, K. (1996) *Divorced, Beheaded, Survived: A Feminist Reinterpretation of the Wives of Henry*

VIII. Reading, Massachusetts: Addison-Wesley Publishing.

- Weir, A. (2011) *Mary Boleyn: The Mistress of Kings*. Ballantine Books.

ADAPTATIONS

- *The Other Boleyn Girl*. (2003) [TV drama]. Philippa Lowthorpe. Dir. UK: BBC.

- *The Other Boleyn Girl*. (2008) [Film]. Justin Chadwick. Dir. UK, US: BBC Films, Relativity Media.

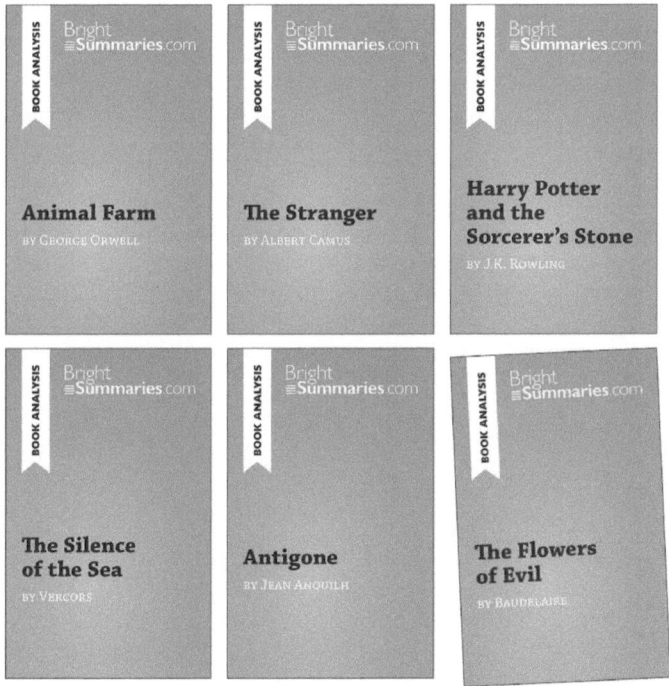

www.brightsummaries.com

Ebook EAN: 9782808017565

Paperback EAN: 9782808017572

Legal Deposit: D/2019/12603/45

Cover: © Primento

Digital conception by Primento, the digital partner of publishers.